ART IN FERMENTED FORM®

A MANIFESTO

BRETT VANDERKAMP

WITH GREG SMITH

ILLUSTRATIONS AND COVER ART BY RICO OUESTE

This is a work of nonfiction.

Illustrations and cover art by Rico Oueste.
Published by Black Lake Press of
Holland, Michigan.

Black Lake Press is a division of
Black Lake Studio, LLC.
Direct inquiries to Black Lake Press at
www.blacklakepress.com.
ISBN 978-0-9883373-4-3

DEDICATION

For my wife, Pam, and my two awe-inspiring boys,
Brayden and Quinn. I wonder every day how
I got so lucky. THANK YOU for always
letting me just be me!

Table of Contents

ACKNOWLEDGEMENTS

There are so many people that I would like to thank for getting me to the place–both physically and emotionally–that I'm in. The last forty years have been a wild ride, and I am thankful that a great group of people has been on it with me:

My family, especially my parents, Steve and Joyce, my grandparents, Doug & Martha VanderKamp and Gene Roedema, my sisters, Megan and Kara, and brother, Joel.

My very supportive in-laws, Jack and Deb Starling.

My mentor Bill Owens, who has helped me to see how far creativity can go.

My assistant Sheila Pollock, who basically keeps me

on course, on time and on message! This book would not have happened with out her.

The incredible team that helped me put this book together. The talented group at Black Lake Press (Greg Smith, Rob Stam, Jami VanderKooi, and Sarah Brummels) for helping me put into words what lives in my soul, and Rick Weese (Rico Oueste) for imagining what those words look like as illustrations.

My "work family" at New Holland–From the people that believed in me in the early days of chasing this dream to the incredibly strong team that is hard at work making the dream come true, a humble and heartfelt "thank you" is all I can say. Let's clap it out!

And finally, to all of the people out there who appreciate the artistry that goes into craft brewing and distilling. Stop and taste, people... stop and taste!

Forward: How to Read this Book

No, I don't mean how to group consonants and vowels together into words and words into sentences and sentences into paragraphs. If you're reading this, then you can already do that.

I mean that this book might not be what you expect. It's not a linear progression of chapters describing the types and science of beer and spirits or the craft brew industry or how to brew your own. It isn't my autobiography or the history of New Holland Brewing.

This book is a non-linear collection of essays about what craft beer and spirits mean to me.

It probably won't shock anyone, but as a guy who

makes his living off beer and spirits, I've had quite a few conversations over a pint—or two. Over the years, I've talked to people from all walks of life and inevitably the same questions come up: *What do you love about beer? Why did you decide to start a brewery? What do you think of mainstream beer? Do you think craft beer has a future with the Big Boy Brews?*

So, it's not really surprising that the format of this book is less than traditional. It's written like all those conversations over the years: spontaneous, passionate, and, yes, sometimes even repetitive.

Feel free to pick it up and set it down a dozen times. Read it out of order. Bend the hell out of the spine. Dog-ear the pages to show to a friend later. Spill beer on it—preferably a fine, hand-crafted brew. Do as you like. This book is yours now. And I hope you will adopt its manifesto as your own: Art in Fermented Form!

My Manifesto

Beer matters.

So do spirits.

Sure, they may not be the most important things in the world, but they changed my life. Through brewing and distilling I discovered history, heritage, and honorable work. I met people, heard their stories, celebrated and mourned with them. They forced me to wrestle with the difference between art and craft, taught me the discipline of someone who makes things with their hands, and commissioned me with the noble task of serving both customers and employees. They have surprised me, delighted me, and honed my creativity to a fine edge—which means that at times they have ground me down, sparks flying in the brewhouse. Beer and spirits have taken me places I never thought that I'd get to go and provided me with a living and recognition. They have also embarrassed me on a few occasions and nearly bankrupted me.

I am a brewer of beer and a distiller of spirits. This is my art, my craft, my profession. I have built a business around learning the secrets of these traditions and imagining ways to create variations on their themes. Anyone who takes up a trade like this becomes shaped by the journey to master it: carpenters and chefs, blacksmiths and builders, painters and playwrights. These are ancient professions, and anyone who takes them up feels the eyes of endless generations of masters watching their work, nodding in approval or shaking their heads as you make the same mistakes they did centuries before.

As an American brewer and distiller, I feel the honor and weight of our particular pedigree: a pedigree rooted in the beer and spirits of mother countries, but with products, techniques, business models, and a drinking culture all our own. Like all American arts and crafts, it integrates and innovates upon the Old World influences. But the history of brewing in America is also a window into the broader history of this country. It is the story of local craftsmen and regionalism, industrialization and commoditization, and finally, a return to local artisanship. Many of the American founding fathers were brewers; their rough hands, fiercely independent spirits, idealistic patriotism, and instinct for commerce are a part of every American pint and dram. Before there was baseball, there was beer. Beer and bourbon are the quintessential American beverages. That's why I age beer in bourbon barrels and bourbon in beer barrels—it is a fusion of our heritage, a celebration of our culture.

Prohibition, beginning on January 16, 1920, lasted 13 years, 10 months, 19 days, 17 hours, 32-1/2 minutes, and was rescinded on December 5, 1933, at 3:32 p.m.

Beer and spirits matter, and they deserve to be taken seriously. That's why this book isn't an educational survey of the craft brewing and distilling industry, a how-to manual for home brewers and would be micro-distillers, or an autobiography of me or my business. All of those types of books are fine, but they don't motivate

PUB

me to read or write, and they certainly don't make me excited about beer, bourbon, and all the products we produce at New Holland Brewing. No, this book is my *manifesto:* a broadside of opinion and a call to action.

So, my fellow connoisseurs, let's rise up and make some demands:

- We will only drink beer and spirits worthy of our traditions and time. Because they matter in general, any specific beer or spirit we drink ought to matter.
- We will drink deliberately, not to get drunk but to celebrate the magic of fermentation and friendship. We will celebrate the quote that is often attributed to Ben Franklin: "Beer is proof that God loves us and wants us to be happy."
- We will expect excellence, insist on creativity, and honor the heritage of brewing traditions. Brewers and distillers are artists and craftsmen!
- We will reject reducing our craft to an industrial commodity. No tasteless beer or rot-gut liquor!
- We will reject innovation for the sake of novelty.
- We will choose to live well, even during tough

times, by being deliberate in what we drink and eat.

Drinkers of the world, unite! Let us live a life less ordinary.

The Anonymous, Happy Straw Man

It was a hot day near the end of a hot summer on the plains of Mesopotamia. Or perhaps it is the steppes of Southern Russia, one of the river valleys of China, or the Zagros Mountains of Iran. Wherever it was, it happened a long time ago, at least 3000 BCE, and probably even earlier.

Ten days before this day, a thunderstorm had blown through the area, knocking over the wild grasses and pummeling the ground with rain so hard that rivulets and deep puddles had formed in the clay-like soil. Then the sun had come out and shone fiercely down on potholes full of rainwater and the floating heads of barley stalks. Some puddles evaporated quickly, but on this spot, a thin grove of cottonwood trees gave enough gauzy cover that the puddles were still half-full.

The oldest known written recipe is for beer.

Today, a few men walk across the field, carrying hunting spears and following a game trail. They wipe the sweat from their brows with their deer hide cloaks, which are pulled back off their shoulders in the heat. When they reach the cottonwoods, they stop to rest. The game has escaped, and they are thirsty. They sit, backs against the tree trunks, and drink from the hide bladders strung around their necks.

One man tips his water bag and utters a curse as he manages to only get a mouthful before it runs dry. In frustration, he leans back against the bark, then looks down. He sees a puddle near his feet, half full of brownish water. His thirst is great enough that he kneels and dips his palms into the puddle. It isn't deep enough for him to get his cupped hands into, so he only wets his tongue. When he does, he stops a moment. The water

looks dirty but tastes strangely sweet. He wants more.

Next to him are some of the downed stalks, and he picks one up. It is about as thick as his little finger and hollow like a tube. He breaks the ends off clean, puts one end into his mouth, and blows the dust and chaff through it. Leaning over the puddle, he dips the other end into the brown water, which is only a couple of inches deep. Tentatively, he sucks through it and draws a mouthful. Again, the water is strangely flavored, bittersweet and heavy, yet pleasant. He takes another sip and finds that it lightens his head in a good way. He likes it and sucks the puddle dry. He sits back against the tree, and the aches and pains in his muscles begin to ease.

He wants more, so he crawls a few feet away to another puddle. He stops and tastes and is delighted to find that it contains more of the wonderful brown water. Now his companions have noticed what he is doing and are laughing at him. He shakes his head and waves them over. He shares his straw and urges one of the others to taste the brown puddle water. His friend's eyebrows shoot up with surprise and delight. A few minutes later, the whole hunting band is crawling around on their hands and knees, sucking from the puddles through their improvised straws.

A few days later, the hunters bring their band to the cottonwood grove, where they set up camp. They begin experimenting, and after a few months, they discover that if they dig holes in the clay, fill them with water and the seeds from the wild barley, then cover the hole with animal hide and wait a week or two, more of the brown water forms.

They have discovered that some plant sugars can undergo spontaneous fermentation due to wild yeasts in the air. More experimentation teaches them to grow the grains intentionally and to carefully remove the seeds. They learn to work with the clay, and they make pots so they don't have to depend on puddles. They figure out how long to let the pots sit, half-buried and covered in the ground outside their tents. Eventually, they learn to speed up the process by cooking the water and grain mixture over the fire, and how to cool it in the evening in a stream. They discover the secret of putting a little bit of the yeast-containing mash from each batch into the next batch to speed the process along.

I don't know who that anonymous, happy straw man was, or where he and his kin lived. But they are my kin, my spiritual ancestors, the first brewers who discovered that the land and elements could be crafted together to make the brown water that makes life a little bit better.

Ben Was Right

Most of us have heard that Benjamin Franklin once said, "Beer is living proof that God loves us and wants to see us happy." Or at least we've been told he said it–I think he was probably saying something about rain, whiskey, and lightning–but whether or not he said it, the truth of the sentiment is not a far stretch. We laugh, hoist our glasses, and cheer his wit.

But Ben had a serious point. Beer is a product of nature. Sun and rain bring green things from the earth. Water and air and tiny creatures come together and make a miracle. Processes too small to see but too powerful to stop rearrange atoms into new molecules that lighten our heads and hearts. Beer and spirits are not made like shoes or swords. Brewers don't assemble beer, and distillers don't manufacture whiskey. These drinks are the harvest of living things, and fermentation is like farming: the crop is cultivated, not controlled.

Brewing demands humility and a reverence for life. It demands respect for the soil and the rhythm of the seasons. When a brewer or distiller lays in a barrel, he or she is capturing a moment, preserving and maturing it for another day. When we raise our glasses, we engage with that other time, with the sun and the barley, the rain and the work of those who brought it all together. Art always connects us to another time and place and gives us perspective—a painting lets us see what people looked like, literature what they thought, architecture how they lived. But the fermented arts let us *taste* last summer or a fall day twelve years past.

As it ages, nearly a third of the whiskey poured into a barrel is lost to evaporation. Distillers refer to this as the "Angels' Share."

Ben was right: this is a blessed magic. The fermented arts are potent reminders that life is a cycle and that

My Manifesto

happiness can be found anywhere if we work with it.

There is an old English folksong that celebrates this miracle, "The Ballad of John Barleycorn." Over the centuries, many poets and songwriters have written variations on it, but the story remains the same. It tells the tale of one John Barleycorn, a symbol for the barley that was the base grain for English beer and spirits. He is ploughed into the soil and clods are piled onto his head. He lies in this grave all winter until:

The cheerful Spring came kindly on,
And showers began to fall;
John Barleycorn got up again,
And sore surprised them all.

The sultry suns of Summer came,
And he grew thick and strong;
His head was armed with pointed spears,
That no one should him wrong.

As summer lapses into autumn, the barley stalks grow pale and droop; John's head is heavy with the grain. Then the farmers unleash their violence upon him, cutting him down at the knees and tying him to a cart. They lay him on his back and beat him, and they hang him up and beat him some more as the grain is separated from the chaff. A miller crushes his bones between two stones as the grain is refined. They put him to the flame, roasting the barley and preparing the malt. Then the brewers fill a dark pit with water and heave him in, and the fermenting process begins. But John Barleycorn's death ultimately brings life:

And they have taken his very heart's blood,
And drank it round and round;
And still the more and more they drank,
Their joy did more abound.

The fermented arts have been woven through civilization from its earliest days. Beer was the first drink (other than water) that played a significant role in human culture. Even today, beer is the world's most widely consumed alcoholic drink, and it is the third most-consumed beverage behind water and tea. This folk song reminds us of how important beer has been to men and women throughout the ages:

John Barleycorn was a hero bold,
Of noble enterprise;
For if you do but taste his blood,
'Twill make your courage rise.

'Twill make a man forget his woe;
'Twill heighten all his joy;
'Twill make the widow's heart to sing,
Though the tear were in her eye.

Ben was right—God gives us the miracle of fermentation to bless our lives, and we should take its happiness seriously. Brewers are the priests who share it with the people, and we should strive to get it right. Ours is a happy art but an art nonetheless. And when we taste John Barleycorn's blood, let us raise our glasses and honor his death that makes our lives so much richer.

Before There Was Baseball, There Was Beer

The Pilgrims may have left England in search of religious liberty, but they stopped at Plymouth Rock because of beer.

They had loaded their ship, the Mayflower, with huge quantities of beer. Having been boiled and then preserved with hops and alcohol, beer was safer to drink than water. The trip across the Atlantic had taken far longer than they had expected, and the passengers and crew were down to their last drops. Although their charter from the government authorized them to plant their colony further south, winds and currents and whatnot meant that it had to be somewhere around Cape Cod or nowhere. But we all know why they stopped early:

they were *running out of freakin' beer!* Massachusetts it would be.

When most British colonists arrived, a brewhouse was one of the first structures they built. Centuries of living in crowded conditions in England had taught them not to drink the water, but beer was boiled, killing most of the bugs. It offered much-needed calories (liquid bread!), relief for aching muscles, and—let's be honest—a welcome little buzz to get you through a hard day of conquering a continent. Long before baseball and apple pie, America ran on beer.

And Americans also loved hard cider. In fact, the apple orchards all over New England weren't originally planted to make pies. Barley didn't grow well there, and hard apple cider was the baseline beverage from Boston to the Berkshires three hundred years ago. Their modern-day descendants might start their day with a venti half-caf double latte, but the flinty Sons of Liberty downed a quart or more of hard apple cider at breakfast before plotting revolution. You can see how that sort of thing could happen.

On the frontier west of the Alleghenies and Appalachians, it was bourbon instead of beer. Barley and apples required clear land, and beer wasn't easily transportable. Cabins and corn could be squeezed into small clearings hacked out of the old growth forests, and corn whiskey was, well, let's just say *efficient*. It didn't take up much room, was easy to carry, and it gave you a pretty good bang for your buck, so to speak. In fact, the pioneers out west called their whiskey "God's Good Creature" because it helped them to cope with the brutal manual labor that life in the middle of nowhere required.

Before the advent of thermometers, brewers tested the temperature of their maturing brews with their thumbs: if it was too cold, the yeast wouldn't grow, and if it was too hot, it would die. This is where we got the term "rule of thumb."

But early American history isn't just a story of beer, cider, and bourbon. All of these were locally crafted products. They had to be because it was impractical to store any of them for long or ship them very far. Early American brewers and distillers were entrepreneurs, small business people whose suppliers and customers were their neighbors. In Europe, the forces of consolidation had been at work for a thousand years; people didn't own their own land, every trade required permission from some nobleman or another, and a thousand lords and ladies had their hands in a tradesman's pocket, taxing away any profit.

From Day One, American brewing and distilling has been a craft culture, practiced by small entrepreneurs buying and selling locally. For a century, the forces of industrialization pushed us away from our heritage. But the craft renaissance of the last twenty years has brought us back to where we began. Where we belong. Where we ought to be. Innovation and independence are bred into our bones.

Will Carrots Make Good Whiskey?

When it comes to fermenting alcoholic beverages, human inventiveness has known no boundaries. I mean that: no boundaries. No. Boundaries. At all. None. As in, humankind will ferment anything. An-y-thing.

The first step is to come up with a base starch, which can be broken down by enzyme activity to produce sugars. These sugars are fermented by yeast to produce alcohol and carbon dioxide. Show me a starch, and I'll show you something that someone somewhere converted to a sugar and used to cop a buzz.

Let's start with how alcoholic beverages get made in the first place. Grapes contain sugar. When they are pressed and stored and yeast is added, the grapes turn into wine. Distill wine and you'll get brandy. Cereal grains are more available in northern climates where grapes don't grow well. Grains like barley can be malted (the germination process of the barley seed is allowed to begin), and an enzyme called amylase breaks down the starches in the endosperm of the seed. Once that happens, we are on our way to whiskey. Malted barley is a more expensive and labor intensive product, and wheat (that hasn't been malted), maize, or rye can be coaxed into producing bourbon, rye, and akvavit. Fruits like apples and peaches can yield brandy, cider, or calvados. Rum can be made from cane sugar. Gin and vodka can be made from cereal grains or potatoes. Japanese sake is made from rice. Tequila uses the sap of the Mexican agave plant, a succulent, as a base starch.

These are all traditional spirits. But now let us now move into darker depths of human imagination. Behold, and marvel at the creative genius of your fellow man...

Kumis is a spirit of the Central Asian steppes, a traditional drink of the Mongol hordes led by Genghis Khan. It is made from fermented mare's milk (as in a female horse). The Greek historian Herodotus mentioned this in the fifth century BCE. *Kumis* should not be confused with *kefir,* a fermented beverage of the

My Manifesto

Russian Caucasus Mountains produced by fermenting cow's, goat's, or sheep's milk with kefir grains.

Advocaat is like a really potent eggnog. It's a Dutch liqueur that's been around since the early 1600s. It is made from brandy, egg yolks, vanilla, cinnamon, and sugar, and has almost the consistency of custard. Yum.

Kvass is also from Russia (apparently, they will do just about anything to get wasted in the frozen wastelands). It uses bread rather than just the base grains as its source of starch. I've never made it, but apparently one pours boiling water over dried bread and then adds a little yeast, molasses, and flour. This mixture is allowed to stand for twelve hours in a warm place, and the microscopic bugs come to life and do their thing. The next morning, you strain the mess and pour it into a bottle, toss in some dried fruit like raisins or apricots, and seal it up for two more days. On the third day, you pour and party. I have actually tried *kvass* and liked it.

I just know that some of you are thinking, "That's all well and good, but what if I'm in prison and really need a drink?" Fear not, because you could make *pruno,* or prison wine. Next time you're in the prison cafeteria trying not to make eye contact with someone scary, stuff some ketchup and sugar packets, an apple, and a slice or two of Wonder Bread into your orange jumpsuit (or wherever you stuff your contraband). Oh yeah, don't forget the plastic bag from–well, from wherever you get plastic bags in prison. When you get back to your cell, and while your roommate is doing pushups, dump all the lunch leftovers in that bag with some hot water (I have no idea how you get hot water, but necessity is the mother of invention, so work it out). Put the bag in your toilet or sink or something for a day or two, and let the magic of fermentation run free. I've heard that *pruno* (also known as *juice, jump, raisin jack, brew, chalk, buck,* and *hooch*) tastes like rotten garbage, but it beats another night on the cell-block stone-cold sober.

You know what else has lots of starch? Organic life forms do–and I don't mean broccoli. Yes, now we come to the deep end of the pool of alcoholic demand, the Marianas Trench of fermentation: animal bodies are full of starch.

Ma zong she chiew is Chinese for–I kid you not–lizard wine, and it is not a metaphor. Apparently, the delicious recipe calls for dropping a couple of lizards or geckos into a clay vat of rice wine along with some ginseng (to help with impotence, or something). Wait twelve months for the lizards to fully ferment into the mixture and then strain out the lovely green liquor. Koreans, on the other hand, eschew bizarre Chinese lizard wines in favor of baby mouse wines. First, drown a large number of baby mice in a vat of rice wine, taking care to use only two- or three-day-old baby mice, commonly called "pinkies," that are still fur-free (hair would throw off the delicate flavor profile). Again, seal and store for a year because it will take you at least that long to work up the courage to smell it, much less drink it. Not to be outdone, South East Asians prefer snake liquors, which they believe cure baldness and, of course, impotence.

But even the Marianas Trench has a deepest point, and that is where we have now arrived. The Eskimos didn't have a lot of starch-giving plants to work with, so let's at least cut them some slack. They would catch a seagull, stuff it into a bottle (don't ask me how, or where they got the bottle), and pour water over it. Then they'd put it out into the sun. Think about it: when the sun shines in the Arctic Circle, it never sets. It just hangs there, low on the horizon, warming the seagull and water mixture, nudging all the starches through the fermentation process until–voila! Hopefully, it was very, very potent.

Rations of rum were given to sailors in the British Army to be mixed with lime juice because it fought off scurvy.

So, will carrots make good whiskey? Carrots contain starch, so there are all sorts of possibilities. We could make a fermented carrot wine and then distill it into carrot brandy. We could also mash the carrots with barley to produce something that is whiskey-like. We could also make a clear grain alcohol and infuse it with carrot flavor, much like juniper is infused into gin, or hops into our New Holland Hopquila.

Would it be whiskey? No. And that raises an interesting set of issues. The names of some spirits are meant to describe fairly specific processes. By law, sparkling white wine can't be called champagne unless it is produced in the Champagne region of France, and barley whiskey can't be called scotch unless it's made in Scotland. I'm not sure if I would call our "carrot liquor," if we ever made such a thing, a whiskey, but it would be fun to try it.

Whiskey and Wood

Could there be whiskey without white oak?

The first documented distillers were Greek scientists in Alexandria during the third century AD, but they wasted the effort on alchemy, not making whiskey. The Arabs who conquered the Mediterranean in the Middle Ages picked up the technique of distilling liquids, but, because they were Muslims, they didn't distill alcohol. By the 1200s, the Italians had figured out that they could distill wine, which they had plenty of, into brandy, which the medieval monasteries used for *purely medicinal purposes* (sure).

A hundred years later the science had spread through the monastery system of Western Europe. In Ireland and Scotland, there were no grapes to distill for brandy, so the monks used barley beer instead. One thing led to another, and whiskey was born. The name is a bastardized English pronunciation of the Gaelic word *uisce,* which meant water. The monks, who spoke Latin, called it *aqua vitae,* the "water of life." The first written record of whiskey is found in the *Annals of Clonmacnoise,* the records of a medieval monastery in central Ireland. It is reported that in 1405, a certain Celtic chieftain drank a bit too much *aqua vitae* at the Christmas feast and promptly expired. In 1495, the financial records of the Scottish government documented that the king sent a shipment of malt to Friar John Cor with an order to make five hundred bottles of aqua vitae because James IV , the king of Scotland at the time, liked scotch whiskey.

When King Henry VIII of England dissolved the monasteries during the Reformation in the 1530s, the monks took their whiskey-making skills into the private sector. Small farms, taverns, and even homes began to distill the water of life. Commercial production was inevitable, and in 1608 the Old Bushmills Distillery on the north coast of Ireland became the first licensed whiskey distillery in the world.

The whiskey of that day was not the wiskey we know today—it hadn't met white oak yet.

Early whiskies were essentially just grain alcohol, distilled to be very potent potables but lacking much flavor because they weren't aged. They were poured into glass bottles or ceramic jugs. Perhaps they found their way into wooden barrels, but only for transport. It never occurred to anyone to let it sit for years and years before drinking. If it sat in glass bottles or ceramic jugs it would eventually go stale, but it wouldn't improve in flavor. If it sat in wooden barrels it would eventually leak out or evaporate, but little flavor would be imparted to it.

You may have come across the word "whisky" spelled "whiskey." It can be quite confusing, but the difference is that the Irish spelled their version "whiskey" while in Scotland they use "whisky." It is generally accepted in the United States that we also spell whiskey with the "e."

Somewhere along the way, there was an unknown traveler. He might have been a monk or a merchant or even a knight. He might have been en route to Rome, or Istanbul, or some other distant land with some *aqua vitae* stored in a barrel fashioned with staves of an oak with a distinctly light color. The months went by; perhaps it took a year or more to complete his journey. When he arrived, the barrels went untapped for another year. Eventually, they were opened.

Our traveler noticed that the barrels were mostly full, but not completely. They hadn't leaked because (unbeknownst to him) the *tyloses* (striations in the cellular structure) in white oak run in two directions, perpendicular to each other. In most trees, even in other oaks, they run in only one direction. But the cross-hatched cellular structure of white oak saturates with liquid, making it both water and rot-resistant. In short, white oak barrels don't leak. However, the tyloses in the white oak barrels had allowed a small amount of the whiskey vapors to evaporate through the wood. This evaporation would soon be known, as it is today, as "the angels' share."

The small share that the angels took allowed a little bit of oxygen into the barrel. This oxidation allowed the alcohol to become infused with some of the flavor of the

My Manifesto

oak. Vanillin and wood tannins imparted character, and oxidation made subtle chemical changes to the liquid.

The result was a whiskey that wasn't just grain alcohol. It had a robust, woody sort of taste to it, with fewer sharp edges. It was good, better than anything our traveler had ever had before. A light bulb went off over his head (which he failed to recognize, since he lived almost five hundred years *before* Thomas Edison), and from that point on, he insisted on aging his aqua vitae in white oak barrels. Thus, the whiskey industry was born.

Generally, whiskey must be aged on wood, although not necessarily in barrels. The industry standard is to use white oak, and in fact United States law requires whiskey to be aged on charred, American white oak for at least two years. The charcoaling process of the wood barrel staves imparts something of the smoky flavor we have come to expect. In Scotland, Scotch whiskey must be aged for at least three years and a day. When we refer to the age of a whiskey (a three-, five-, or twelve-year-old bottle, for example), we refer to the length of the barrel aging, not how long it has been since it was bottled. In general, the longer it lives in the white oak, as the angels take their little sips and the tyloses force wood and whiskey to merge, the more round and complex the spirit will be.

White oak and whiskey need each other. We have to wait patiently until they finish their work. So, would we have whiskey without white oak? You tell me!

Arts and Crafts

When I was a student at Hope College, which is across the street from where our pub now stands, I minored in sculpture. I've always loved shaping raw materials to make a tangible thing that resembles something from my imagination. In my design classes, I first heard the endless debate about what can be called "art" and what is merely "craft."

This debate has been raging since ancient times. Some people think it's a pointless argument about semantics and couldn't care less, but I think it matters because I want to create things that really matter. I work hard at what I do, and I want to measure the reality of my accomplishments against the idealism of my ambitions. New Holland is a craft brewery and distillery, and we believe that we are creating art in fermented form. We are convinced that this is the ultimate art project. Are we deluding ourselves?

Bourbon is the official alcohol of the United States, by an act of Congress. Over the years, many people have attempted to have that overturned in favor of beer.

"Craft" is generally understood as the art of making practical things. "Art" is generally understood as using craft to express something important, which has inherent, even transcendent, worth beyond what you can do with it. Craft is about functionality; it measures success by how useful the product is. One of the measures of art is that it is valuable without being needed. Craft is painting a wall so the room can be enjoyed; art is VanGogh painting "A Starry Night" on canvas.

But the line between art and craft is not always sharp or bright. I remember being assigned to design and build a chair in one of our college sculpture classes. At first glance, furniture building seems to be a craft: you want

a chair to be attractive, but it must hold your weight, be comfortable, affordable, etc. On the other hand, can a chair be conceived with such genius and crafted with such grace that it becomes art? On the first day of the project, the professor showed us the raw materials—wood, glue, fabric, nails—and told us to imagine the nearly infinite ways they could be combined to make a beautiful thing that one could sit on. In the end, my chair wasn't particularly beautiful or comfortable. It fell into an awkward valley between craft and art, rising to neither.

But that professor's words have stuck in my mind. When we started New Holland, we wanted to master the brewer's craft and work the artist's magic. Our beers and spirits are always measured practically (do people enjoy drinking them?), and our audience votes with its wallet. But when I stand in the brewery and stillhouse and look at the raw materials—barley, hops, water, and flavor ingredients—I try to imagine the nearly infinite ways that they can be combined to make something that elevates the drinking experience and expresses something unique and important through it.

Will You Like It?

Marketers like to talk about a "brand promise:" the commitments that a seller makes to the buyer or what the consumer can expect from his product. When we started New Holland Brewing, we were tempted to build a brand that implied that anyone who tried our beer would like it. For young people who were taking enormous financial risks, it only made sense to guarantee that our brews would be drinkable and enjoyable from the first sip. The safest strategy would have been to make our pub and brews exactly what consumers expected so that no one would be disappointed on their first visit.

But while it might have been the smart play, it wasn't the right thing to do. West Michigan didn't need just another bar serving up the same drinks with a different label. If our core product was predictable, we would be forced to compete on price or location or ambiance, but we didn't want New Holland Brewing to be about discounts and décor–we wanted it to be about the beer. That meant brewing creatively, striving to be remarkable by pursuing art in fermented form. Artists might *try* to guarantee that people will like what they offer, but no artist can. Art takes risks in pursuit of vision and strives for a particular expression of that vision.

Whiskies do not mature in the bottle, only in the cask, so the "age" of a whiskey is the time between distillation and bottling.

We have always worked to create beers that have a unique signature that embody our insight into a tradition or style. We had to be willing to take the chance that a consumer might order a pint, take a sip, make a face, and say, "No, that is not for me." Our Dragon's Milk is not like the stout a consumer is used to ordering at a chain restaurant. Our Blue Sunday Sour is probably unlike anything the average customer has ever tasted

B
C

before, and our Hatter Royale surprises everyone with its composition and taste. Our products are often unexpected, and not everyone will like all of them.

So if our brand promise is not "*You will like it,*" then what is it? This is our commitment: *If you stop, taste our beer, and give it your attention, you will be surprised and be taken somewhere you didn't expect.*

Of course, some people don't want to go on a journey when they order a drink. They want to pay their money and get poured something they like, but I've always wondered about people who are overly sure of what they do and don't like. We respond to art in context, depending on our mood and circumstances. Think about your music collection for a moment. You might have dozens of genres, hundreds of artists, and thousands of songs. Which is your favorite? Which do you want to listen to all the time? If you're like me, none are your favorite, and every song in your collection is there because, at one time or another, it just seemed right.

Every beer we ferment and every spirit we distill is trying to say something, and on any given day, every one of them can be the right or wrong drink. You may not like it now, and that's just fine. But listen to it, learn something from tasting it, and file it away. There may come a time and a place where it's just right.

Cheers, Sláinte, Tchin-tchin, Opa!

Beer has always brought people together.

Beer is a communal beverage. The first graphic images we have of beer drinking are Mesopotamian, from approximately 2000-2500 BCE. They all depict people sitting or standing around a large jar on the floor, drinking beer from it with long straws (three or four feet long). They are looking at each other, obviously in conversation.

It takes a village to pour a beer; farmers, brewers, merchants, tavern owners all contribute to the process. And while the ingredients or the brews themselves have always been stored in some fashion or another so they can be consumed throughout the year, they are by nature products of the harvest. It was the communal effort of the harvest that transformed humans from hunter-gatherers to farmers and civilization from nomadic tribes to villagers and city-dwellers. Nomads could have meat and cheese and were able to bake bread over a campfire, but the process of brewing beer required settling down and working together in harmony with the rhythm of the seasons.

Before bottling and pasteurization made it possible for beer to be an individual drink, it was consumed with others, originally from jars, as in those ancient Mesopotamian drawings, and later from barrels and taps. In the ancient world, women brewed in the home and served beer with family meals—it was safer to drink than water and eased muscles worn from physical labor. But people drank beer together in palaces and taverns as well, from straws and cups. In fact, inns and taverns were places were the community gathered at the end of the day and travelers rested on their journey. That's the origin of the word "pub," short for "public house," a place where the public gathered in the days before telephones and televisions to meet and talk, to share local news, to hear from travelers what was happening in the wider world, and to celebrate as well as mourn.

My Manifesto

It played such a central role in the fabric of community life. In the eighteenth-century-BCE Code of Hammurabi (the first known set of written laws), tavern owners who overcharged for their beer were to be put to death by drowning.

Cenosillacaphobia: fear of an empty glass.

And not to ignore the obvious, the intoxicating effect of beer loosens our tongues, breaks down barriers, lowers our inhibitions, and brings our emotions to the surface. All of that can be for better or worse, of course. But because beer has a lower alcohol content than spirits, we tend to sit longer and talk more as we drink it. A few pints, whether sipped from a jar through a four-foot straw or from individual mugs, set almost the perfect pace for a meal and conversation. From the time of Hammurabi in the Fertile Crescent (and probably before), beer has been a catalyst for fellowship with family and friends.

That's why every language has a word or phrase

that means something like, "A toast to your health!" In England it is *Cheers!* In Ireland, it's *Sláinte* (which just means "health" in Gaelic). Albanians say *Gëzuar* ("enjoy"). The Germans and Dutch say *Prost* (from Latin, "May it be good for you"). In Wales, *Iechyd Dda* ("good health"), in Vietnam, *Chuc suc khoe* ("good health to you/us"). In Hebrew, *l'chaim* ("to life"). And in Italy and France they say *tchin-tchin* to mimic the sound of two classes clinking together. When we gather to hoist a glass and say a toast in whatever language we speak, we are participating in one of mankind's oldest cultural rituals. Since at least four or five thousand years ago (and probably earlier than that), men and women have come together and done the same thing and wished their drinking mates well.

We think about that at New Holland. It's why we want to get this most enduring marker of civilization right. Good beer and great spirits, brewed or distilled and drinking deliberately with friends, unites us not only with those at the table but also with our companions across time and space.

Concealed Carry? Hell Yes, I'm Packing!

W.C. Fields, the Vaudeville comedian who starred in films during the 1920s and 30s, always carried a hip flask. When people would ask him if he really needed to be carrying alcohol around all the time, he would maintain that it contained nothing more than pineapple juice. One day while he was on a film set, a prankster snuck into his dressing room, emptied his flask, and refilled it with pineapple juice. Later, after the day's shooting had finished and the cast had changed back out of costume, Fields pulled out his flask and took a little tug.

"*Phew!*" he said, spitting it out and looking suspiciously at the cast and crew, "What rascal has been putting pineapple juice into my pineapple juice?!"

❧ ☙

In 1788, Ale was proclaimed "the proper drink for Americans" at a parade in New York City. In English pubs, ale is ordered by pints and quarts. So in old England, when customers got unruly, the bartender would yell at them to mind their own pints and quarts and settle down. It's how we got the phrase "mind your P's and Q's."

❧ ☙

Hip flasks for spirits (usually, but not always, whiskey) are of dubious legality in most of the United States. During Prohibition, the state of Indiana made them illegal to own. They are still considered "open containers" of alcohol; if you get busted with one in the passenger compartment of your car or on your person as you walk down most streets, you will be getting a ticket (or worse). Sports stadiums and restaurants hate them, not because they are illegal but because places that make money selling you drinks aren't cool with BYOB (please

don't bring flasks into my brewpub just to test me!).

But beyond legality and commercial rules, flasks are anathema to our culture's current attitude toward alcohol. While craft brewing and artisan distilling have gone mainstream, and folks with bucks to spend now go on whiskey tours in the Highlands of Scotland like people used to tour the wine regions of France, there are still taboos. Pulling out a flask and having a nip in most social settings (graduations, weddings, funerals, etc.) is sure to get you disapproving stares at best, and probably a scathing lecture. You certainly won't be invited back. You'll be considered a dirty alcoholic, a cautionary tale, only a few refills away from urinating in alleys and exposing yourself on subways. For most of us, the only socially acceptable place to whip out a flask is in a golf cart (but not at the company outing) or on a ski lift.

Which is why I love the idea of owning one. It's a statement of defiance, a sort of middle-finger-extended-but-still-in-the-pocket to the social conformity of the Nanny State that assumes it can approve my choices. The Nanny State will pay for all sorts of things that I find objectionable, but it frowns upon me carrying a flask of Beer Barrel Bourbon to have a wee nip during coffee break at the conference. The concealed and carried flask—whether I choose to sip or not—is my silent act of disrespect for political correctness. A little Walden Cabin in my pocket.

And what has politcal correctness done for us lately? Hey, I watched the series *Mad Men*: the "Greatest Generation" had wet bars in their offices and drank Scotch during meetings—and they defeated the Nazis, built the interstate highways, and launched the electronic age! We persecute anyone who even looks fondly on a trans fat, we can't fix the potholes, and we are running up a $92 gazillion deficit handing out government cell phones. Every time I get irritated, I reach in my jacket and touch my flask. I feel like Winston Smith in *1984*, fondling the stolen memo that proved Big Brother was full of crap.

I don't condone or encourage irresponsible drinking, much less alcoholism or debauchery. But I do think that a flask is a marvelous gift for a friend and a quiet symbol of civil disobedience. If you give a friend a flask, maybe have it engraved with something poignant (like an Irish blessing) or witty (like *This End Up,* or *Pineapple Juice,* or *This is Mine, Make Your Own*), and fill it with an artisan spirit from New Holland Brewing.

During World War II, the Royal Air Force used "hip flask" as a radio code for a pilot's revolver. Perhaps the readers of this book could adopt our own code: "Are you carrying?"

I remember a stark, winter's day in 1998, a year after we opened our brewpub. On that cold Saturday, we unlocked the doors and waited for the customers. And waited. And waited some more. We didn't have a single customer that day. None. Holland, Michigan was (and still is) a quiet, conservative, deeply religious town. There were a couple of bars, but they were crappy and served crappy beer. We were trying to introduce craft brewing to a culture that banned beer sales on Sunday for crying out loud. I remember walking outside and shouting my feelings toward the downtown area, middle fingers raised.

I might have been a bit immature in how I handled that situation. Now that I'm older and wiser, I just touch the flask in my pocket and keep my mouth shut.

Henry Ford Didn't Make Beer

...nor would he have, as the nation's first large-scale industrial manufacturer was a "teetotaler." Teetotalers were the driving force behind Prohibition, which made beer and spirits illegal in the United States between 1920 and 1933. The name referred to their commitment to refrain from alcohol *totally*—"T for Total" became *teetotaler*. Not only did Henry completely abstain from alcohol, he also insisted that all his employees at the Ford Motor Company do the same. He created an in-house "Sociological Department" to spy on Ford workers, with the power to drop by for unexpected inspections of their homes. If they discovered alcohol or detected it on an employee's breath, even outside work hours, he was fired on the spot. In fact, during Prohibition, Henry Ford declared that, "If booze ever comes back to the United

States, I am through with manufacturing...I wouldn't be interested in putting automobiles into the hands of a generation soggy with drink." The *New Yorker* magazine, noting Detroit's reputation as a smuggling center for bootleg liquor from nearby Canada, wrote that, "It would be a great pity to have Detroit's two leading industries destroyed in one blow."

Ford was an innovator in mass manufacturing, using the latest principles in assembly lines, interchangeable parts, industrial organization, and commercial distribution to sell a standardized product, the automobile, to the general public. Local or regional craft manufacturers could never compete with the uniform quality, low cost, and aggressive marketing efforts of the scale that Ford brought to the automobile. By 1918, half of all the cars in the US were Model Ts.

But all of them were the *same*. Ford famously explained his philosophy as, "Any customer can have a car painted any color that he wants, so long as it is black."

Ironically, while Henry Ford wouldn't manufacture beer or spirits, his innovations surely influenced them for the rest of the twentieth century. Brewing and distilling

had always been the work of craftsmen and artisans. The ingredients were grown locally, since shipping and storage were expensive. For the same reason, they were largely consumed locally as well (although spirits could be stored longer and shipped more economically because of their smaller volume). Local ingredients made by local production methods and created by local tastes produced brews and liquors with distinctly local styles and flavors.

A barrel contains 31 gallons of beer. What Americans commonly refer to as a keg is actually 15.5 gallons, or a half-barrel.

But the lessons learned by Ford and others who followed in his footsteps quickly changed what Americans (and others around the world) expected from consumer products. The world wars, urbanization, and prosperity led to the mass manufacture and marketing of almost everything consumers drove, used, wore, and ate. Gone were the local butcher and baker; in their places were Spam and Wonder Bread. This wasn't all bad, of course—

none of us wants to ride in a one-off airliner or use a craft computer—but it definitely changed the American diet and lifestyle for the worse.

Beer and spirits became mass produced. The timing of industrialization, coinciding with Prohibition, followed by the Depression, followed by World War II—doomed craft brewers and artisan distillers. The result was standardized, watery beer because it was cheaper and easier to make, ship, and sell on a national scale. Canned beer was stacked in hot trucks and on grocery store shelves for months next to disposable diapers and boxes of macaroni and cheese.

Industrialized food and drink have some real drawbacks, such as:

- In order to achieve standardization and a longer shelf life, the manufacturing process strips out many of the organic nutrients and compounds. Besides affecting nutrition, these are the very qualities that impart flavor profiles to products.
- The emphasis on quantity and cost over quality and local connection has led to high calorie consumption. It's been a double-edged sword: cheap food has largely meant an end to large-

scale hunger in the industrialized world, but now the poor are fat. For the first time in history, obesity is becoming a mark of poverty.

- Severing the relationship between consumers and the sources of their food and drink has destroyed local economies.
- Local texture and regional character has been steamrollered. There is a boring sameness to what we eat and drink across the United States.

But the tide is turning: there are now over two thousand craft breweries in the United States (forty per state, on average), the most since the 1880s. This renaissance in craft beer and artisan spirits is about reclaiming what is essential to our DNA as brewers and drinkers. It is about rejecting the notion that our pint or shot should be reduced to the lowest common denominator that can be made and sold to the millions. Customization is the opposite of industrial scaling, and eating and drinking locally is helping us to restore a more traditional relationship with food and drink that makes life healthier and more enjoyable.

THE PURITY OF THE PINT

It sits there, a cylinder dripping with condensation. It bleeds a wet ring onto the wood, blending into the thousands left by other customers, other conversations. Complicated physics regulate the ratio between its foamy head and slowly flattening body, but only physicists would care, and most of them would rather sip it than calculate. In the minds of many, it is wine's less-sophisticated cousin from the countryside, but its flavors are more complex than any glass of wine, which can boast of only one ingredient. This pint of beer, on the other hand, took a cookbook to create. It is a fusion of all the ancient elements: fire and water, earth and air. It is the universe in a glass.

What does the pint offer? What does it demand?

Some find a devil in its depths. In his international bestseller *Angela's Ashes,* Frank McCourt describes growing up in Limerick, Ireland during the Great Depression, and the fearsome hold that the pint had on his father. When his uncle takes Frank out for his coming-of-age-first-pint-at-a-local-pub, his toast testifies to the power of the pint to bless or curse:

> *The barman brings the pints, Uncle Pa pays, lifts his glass, tells the men in the pub, This is my nephew Frankie McCourt, son of Angela Sheehan, the sister of my wife, having his first pint, here's to your health and long life Frankie, may you live to enjoy the pint but not too much.*

Yes, the pint can be a blessing or a curse. It has no power in itself, but only what we give to it. We can enjoy it, and some enjoy it too much. We rob its potential when we reduce it to a delivery system for alcohol, a tool of intoxication. It can be so much more if we demand that it be, if we will expect art and accept nothing less.

The pint is a product of the brewer's palette. It can be complex because there are so many colors the brewer can arrange in seemingly endless combinations. The flavor begins with ingredients: barley malt and hops plus a universe of other possibilities to shape its profile (everything from barley to pumpkin and wheat to coffee). The flavor is further honed by how and how long the brewer chooses to age it—for example, we age our Dragon's Milk in bourbon barrels to impart a unique flavor, and we allow wild yeasts in our Blue Sunday Sour to further break down the alcohol into acids which give it a, well, sour flavor. What color will it be? Color may not affect the taste buds, but it certainly shapes how we experience it. And let us not forget temperature (during fermentation, storage, and serving) as another tool in the brewer's box. How will it be stored and shipped? In barrels, casks, kegs, bottles, cans? All of those affect taste. How will it be presented? In what sort of glassware? The shape matters, as does cleanliness, and some detergents leave a residue that affects taste. In what quantity? To be sipped or quaffed? Paired with what foods?

Monks brewing beer in the Middle Ages were allowed to drink five quarts of beer a day.

In fact, this is one of the differences between beer and wine or spirits. While the flavors in wine can also be complex, they are not as versatile because wine has fewer variables: one ingredient, less steps in the process, and fewer choices in presentation. As for spirits, the targets are tighter: while there are many ways to make whiskey, there are more to make beer. So, more than any of these other drinks, a poured pint is the brewer's interpretation of beer, like a jazz musician's improvisational riffs upon the basic theme of a song.

That's all well and good for the brewer, but what are *our* expectations for the pint? What shall we ask–no, demand–of it for we bring our own variables into play. Where are we hoisting it? Who are we with? When? What mood are we in, and what's on our schedule afterward? Are we hungry? What foods are we pairing it with? Are we focused on our pint, or are we engaged in something else while we drink? All of this matters because it dictates what we ask of it, how we engage with it.

The brewer paints his pint, and we engage with it. Some beers are more approachable and ask less of the drinker. A decent, drinkable IPA asks less of you, whereas a more subtle and complex pint requires you to focus—it doesn't come to you, you have to go to it. I enjoy an easy beer as much as the next person, but I believe that real art requires your attention. You will never understand a great piece of art if you are distracted—that's why gallery walls are usually bare around the paintings.

Dragon's Milk is, perhaps, the best known member of our High Gravity Series. I believe it is a serious beer. It allows for no distractions. It demands your deliberate attention. Its flavors are complex, and to really appreciate them, it has to be served in very particular ways and drunk deliberately. It is not a beer to be enjoyed in a large plastic cup while sitting in the bleachers over third base under a hot sun in the sixth inning while you wait for a foul ball to come your way. We brew a couple of beers that would be perfect for that situation, but Dragon's Milk is not one of them.

All this is to say that the "perfect beer" is always a moving target because it is always a perfect intersection between the brewer's choices and yours. Today it might be Dragon's Milk; tomorrow it might be Mad Hatter. There is no absolute truth, except that lazy brewers and lazy drinkers deserve each other.

Don't misunderstand me: there is too much to be done in this world to turn making and drinking beer into a chore. It shouldn't be intimidating to pick the perfect pint to enjoy at that moment. We should think of it as an opportunity to discover and delight in the richness of life.

The Subtlety of Spirits

One of the recurring categories on the game show *Jeopardy* was "Potent Potables." A potent potable is an alcoholic beverage, and let's face it, some of them are more potent than others. Beer and wine make you feel fine, but hard liquors pack a punch. This creates opportunities for those that make, drink, and mix them. Wild stallions can be hard to tame, but if distillers, bartenders, and chefs make shrewd use of the intense qualities that spirits offer, all sorts of interesting tastes and experiences can be created. The key is to control their firepower and direct it at will. Whiskeys, gins, vodkas, rums, and all the rest of the distilled spirits can have very subtle qualities, which can be appreciated straight or combined in an infinite number of cocktails. *I'll take "Potent Potables" for $1,000, Alex!*

Let's define our terms. Alcoholic beverages can be divided into two broad categories: those that were produced *only* by fermentation of sugars (wine and beer), and fermented beverages that went through an extra process of distillation to increase the percentage of alcohol to at least twenty percent of volume. This second category is known as spirits, liquors, or sometimes hard liquors. Since beers are generally between four and ten percent alcohol by volume, even the tamest spirits are two, three, or four times more powerful for the amount. Some are considerably more.

In the United States, the term "proof" is defined as twice the percentage of alcohol by volume (ABV). So a spirit or liquor that is 20% ABV is labeled "40 proof." Legend has it (I have no idea if this is true, but I've heard it many times and it sounds good, so I'm going with it) that the term "proof" originated in the British Navy in the 1700s. The sailors were paid partially in rum (are you feeling this?). However, the sailors were a suspicious lot, and they suspected the Navy of being sneaky and watering down their rum allotments. To guarantee that it hadn't been, the rum was "proved" by dipping a little bag of gunpowder in the rum barrel. Once the gunpowder was wet with rum, it was laid on a table

or deck of the ship and a match was put to it. If the rum had been so watered down that it contained less than about 57% alcohol by volume, the gunpowder wouldn't catch the spark. If it did burn—if it was 57% ABV—then they had "one hundred percent proof" that the rum was real. Over the last couple of centuries, mathematical shenanigans have led to the standard that 50% ABV is 100 proof.

All this is to say that the high ABV of spirits can make the distiller's job either easier or more difficult, depending on his objective. If he just wants the consumer to get intoxicated efficiently, then his task is simple: keep the ABV high and the price low. A lot of rot-gut liquor is made, sold, and drunk under exactly that model. But if the distiller wants to create interesting flavors and experiences, he has to work a little bit harder. The taste and effects of the alcohol can overwhelm subtle ingredients and techniques. Whiskey, for example, can have profiles as complex as any beer or wine, but the taste buds can be overloaded and the mind dulled too quickly to appreciate them unless the distiller, drinker, and bartender work together to manage the experience. They have to be mindful of the ingredients and more deliberate in how they go about making, mixing, or drinking.

When we launched our New Holland Artisan Spirits line, I had two goals. First, I wanted to begin moving toward a more holistic, local approach to spirits. I wanted to see how far we could go in using local or regional ingredients and methods to produce spirits that honored but innovated upon the heritage of American whiskeys, rums, gins, and vodkas. I think we've created products that have a unique, Great Lakes pedigree, and we've been able to re-imagine some classics—like our Hatter Royale, which is a grain-based but tequila-tasting spirit that bridges our brewing and distilling operations. In the same spirit, our Beer Barrel Bourbon is aged in our used Dragon's Milk barrels, creating an interesting fusion of our product flavors.

Second, and more importantly, I wanted to make spirits that managed the alcohol-flavor balance so well that they didn't overload the taste buds. Our spirits are drinkable because they're tasteable. The consumer can detect what's going on in them and what we were trying to do. They aren't just booze in a bottle that burns the tongue as it clouds the mind.

I remember going into a bar in Austin, Texas a few years ago. I had gotten into town that afternoon, and wanted to check out the famous scene on Sixth Street.

I went into one bar and the tender asked me, "So, what can I get you?"

"I'm not sure. I just got here. What do you recommend?"

She leaned forward thoughtfully. "Tell me more. Have you been traveling all day?"

"Yeah, I just got off the plane from Michigan a couple of hours ago."

"Hmmm," she said. "Tell me more. How are you feeling? What are your plans later?"

She asked me a whole series of questions. She wanted to know what sort of mood I was in, how tired or energetic I felt, how late I planned on being out that night, whether I had already eaten dinner or would be eating later. What kinds of liquors did I like, with what sort of profiles? She knew that she could combine dozens of ingredients into hundreds or thousands of variations, and she wanted to get it just right. The right liquor, mixed the right way, for me that night. That's the way it should be done.

࿐ ࿐

Single Malt Whiskey comes from a single distillery and a single grain. However, it is possible that it underwent maturing in multiple casks.

࿐ ࿐

Because of that, I don't want New Holland's spirits sold at the "speed rail" in bars. A speed rail is rack along the bar that holds the bottles the bartender will use most in a night. For convenience, it's right in front of him or her, so drinks can be poured quickly as they are ordered. But that's not where I want our liquors located. That's counterintuitive, because if our motivation was purely financial then we'd want them in the bartenders hands with every drink he pours. But the speed rail is full of less interesting, nearly generic, low-cost brands that get tossed in cocktails that overwhelm the flavor of the spirit. They're commodities. If I had my way there would be no speed rails at all, and bartenders would be more deliberate in choosing the right spirit for the customer. But if there must be house-liquors, let our products be proudly up on the shelf behind the bar where they will be called for and hopefully suggested.

I want our Artisan Spirits to have stand-alone character. That doesn't mean that everyone will drink them straight, but when used in cocktails I want the flavor of the spirit to rise above the juices, sodas, and syrups they are blended with. I hate cocktails where I can't taste the foundational liquors, where the only contribution of the spirit is the alcohol. I hope that when people mix a cocktail with our products, they will ease off the other ingredients just a bit and appreciate the personality of the liquor.

When I was a senior in college, a couple of my friends and I held a party at which there would be plenty of "potent potables." Getting college kids to show up and drink free liquor may very well be the easiest thing I've ever done in my life. But that night, I wanted to slow people down a little bit, make them think and be a little more creative and deliberate. So I stood at the door and told them that there was a cost to get in. They looked at me, confused for a moment, and then looked past me to all the bottles on the table. I heard over and over again, "Uh, I don't have any money with me..."

"No, the cost isn't cash," I would explain. "You have

to give me a quote to get in."

"A quote? I don't get it"

"A quote," I said, "like from a famous person. You could say, 'We have nothing to fear but fear itself,' or 'Give me liberty or give me death,' or 'Golf is a good walk spoiled.' It doesn't matter. Just come up with a quote and write it on one of these slips of paper. Later on, we're going to read them. It will be interesting."

Over and over, I got blank stares. I turned away more than half of the people that came to our door that night. These were students in a private, liberal arts college. They should have been able to think of *something*. But they were so intent on getting inside and guzzling cheap alcohol that all their imagination and recollection had evaporated.

I think that's what so many of us do today with spirits. We aren't curious about our cocktails and we don't want to stop and taste what's in them. We just want them to punch us so we can party.

I want to make spirits that help reconnect the drink to the drinking experience, and make it all much more deliberate so that we can rediscover all the possibilities in our "potent potables."

The Promise of the Publican

Stop me if you've heard this one: a priest, a rabbi, and a minister walk into a bar...

Or maybe it's a republican and a democrat, or a pirate and an astronaut. There are a thousand variations on that basic joke because other than churches, few places have been more central to the life of a community than its pub (or tavern or bar). Whatever you call it, since the earliest man brewed beer, there has been somewhere to drink it, meet others, and either talk, barter, or fight.

In the Anglo-American tradition, the earliest watering holes were Roman *tabernae,* which sat at the crossroads of the Roman roads across the British landscape. After the Romans left, the Saxons came, and *tabernae* morphed into alehouses. Women brewed ale

at home, but over time some private homes became *public houses,* or pubs for short, where neighbors could meet to buy a pint of ale and a bite to eat while gossiping and informally conducting business.

The traditional English pub had several rooms. The saloon was the fanciest space in the pub and often featured entertainment, with a cover charge for admission or reserved for community VIPs and sometimes club members. The public bar was the larger open space for community eating and drinking. "The snug" was a small room for private parties and confidential conversation. The life of the neighborhood flowed through these rooms in the days before television, telephones, and Internet—much less the automobile and electric lights.

In America, drinking was an important part of daily life. Fermented or distilled beverages were considered safer to drink than water, and alcohol was valued for its pain-killing and medicinal qualities. In fact, Americans drank a lot, and I do mean *a lot.* In the years leading up to the American Revolution, rum was cheap in the colonies because of the busy trade routes running between the Atlantic seaports and the sources of sugarcane in the Caribbean. Beer was locally produced, and taverns were an important part of the American colonial culture.

People ate and drank in the taverns, of course, but they also conducted business, got their mail, and held political meetings. The Continental Congress, which would eventually commission and sign the Declaration of Independence, held its first gathering in City Tavern in Philadelphia, and the same year, the United States Marine Corps was formed across town in Tun Tavern.

In fact, the great eighteenth-century English writer and statesmen Samuel Johnson often waxed poetic about how much he loved hanging out in the pub: "There is nothing which has yet been contrived by man, by which so much happiness is produced as by a good tavern or inn." Nothing? Well, writers are often given to hyperbole.

The word "bridal" comes from 19th century Englishmen, who took out their mates for a final "Bride Ale" the day before their wedding.

I have a lot of opinions about pubs because in addition to being a brewer and distiller, I am a publican.

Not a *re*publican, but a publican, the old English term for a pub owner.

When we moved New Holland's brewpub into our current location, I wanted to rethink the design model. We bought a historic building on the busiest corner in downtown Holland, Michigan. Throughout most of its life, the building has housed retail stores—a department store, a hardware emporium. For that reason, it had large plate glass windows facing the sidewalk and the corner. They were perfect for looking inside to see the merchandise, but this raised some real concerns for our pub. Holland had been a very conservative, religious town, and our location was just a block away from a Christian college. Some people were worried that customers might not want passersby to see them through the windows, drinking in a bar. Would that exposure keep customers away? Should we cover the windows?

I felt strongly that we should not. It seemed important to me to make a point from our first day in the new location: our pub would be a true public house, a place where the community gathered, a place to people watch and to be seen. The windows were not an inconvenience; they were essential.

Just last week I got an email from a downtown business leader:

Just wanted to share with you how much success I believe you have achieved in making the NHBC pub a place where ideas and positive social interaction regularly occur. This struck me last night after leaving two insightful and beneficial conversations at neighboring high tops with people I hadn't previously met. Both imparted useful knowledge that will be helpful in my work.

You have told me that one of the goals in founding the pub with huge windows was to make it a community gathering place for commerce in the exchange of ideas.

You've achieved it–as those who come regularly make so plain.

Kudos, cheers.
Jim.

There are a lot of commercial pressures that work against the kind of pub we'd like to have. The modern restaurant business operates on very narrow margins. We don't make money from patrons lingering in endless conversation over nearly empty glasses. Each table has to generate a certain amount of revenue per hour, so there is a real need to turn the tables and seat new parties. It can easily become a consumption experience rather than a community gathering place. I often wonder: is it possible to keep our ideals and still be profitable?

Lately, I find myself contemplating the saloon and the snug, those exclusive rooms in the traditional English pub. Would it be possible to set aside an area for customers who want a more deliberate experience? An area in the pub where there is less pressure to consume quickly and clear out for the next party? A space dedicated to more deliberate drinking and conversation?

As a publican, I make you this promise: we will always do everything we can to create a focal point for the community, a place to meet and greet. I promise to create the kind of place that Samuel Johnson described:

> *As soon as I enter the door of a tavern, I experience an oblivion of care, and a freedom from solicitude: when I am seated, I find the master courteous, and the servants obsequious to my call; anxious to know and ready to supply my wants: wine there exhilarates my spirits, and prompts me to*

free conversation and an interchange of discourse with those whom I most love: I dogmatize and am contradicted, and in this conflict of opinion and sentiments I find delight.

Our brewpub is ready. Stop by and taste what we've created.

WHEN BREWERS JUMP THE SHARK

I've already pointed out that throughout history, people have fermented some outrageous things to get a buzz. Necessity is the mother of invention, after all. But what are we to make of "beard yeast" beer? This is a real thing, and not in some Panamanian prison or Siberian village. There is a craft brewing company (I won't mention its name) that is fermenting its beer with yeast from the brewmaster's beard. Apparently, the dude has been growing the beard since the 1970s—it's an "old growth beard"—and he took some hair follicles from his chin, stuck them in a petri dish, and yeast developed. They thought it would be clever to brew with it.

Here's my question: when does creativity give way to novelty? When does innovation give rise to art, and when has it descended to silly gimmicks to grab attention? In this book I've celebrated several times that we now have over two thousand craft breweries in America. While we are seemingly nowhere close to meeting consumer demand, it does make it hard to get noticed. And in the craft beer industry, as in high school, nothing will get you noticed quite as much as being outrageous.

One of the most popular television series' of the 1970s was "Happy Days." It was about a gang of teenagers living in Milwaukee during the 1950s (portrayed by actors in their thirties). The star of the show was Fonzie, a tough biker in a leather jacket who was the coolest dude anyone knew. The show was enormously successful, but by the fifth season the writers were out of ideas for storylines. To prop up weak ratings, they came up with a multiple-part episode in which the characters took a trip to Hollywood. Inevitably, they ended up on the beach, and for some reason the writers thought it would be clever and funny to have Fonzie go waterskiing in his leather jacket. As he zoomed along, mugging for the camera, an enormous rubber prop shark floated up in his path while the soundtrack turned menacing. But Fonzie was the coolest guy around, so he didn't overreact. He just jumped over the shark and kept on going in his leather jacket and board shorts. Since then, "jumping the shark"

has become a way to describe that awkward moment when something has run out of ideas and is desperately crying for help.

~

12 oz. of a typical American pale lager actually has fewer calories than 2% milk or apple juice.

~

Not to pick on beard yeast beer, but craft brewers have to resist the temptation to create products that attract attention just because they are shocking or a joke. It might give a brand a quick bump ("Happy Days" shot up in the ratings for a little while, mostly because the audience said *WTF was that?*), but at what cost? Novelty products don't advance our art, create authentic consumer experiences, or build long-term trust in a brand.

We need brewers and distillers to think outside the box and experiment. But do we really need banana bread beer? What about doughnut bacon maple ale? Those are actual products, but are they just creative experiments or novelty gimmicks? Someone is brewing chili beer, pizza beer, and a stout that tastes like s'mores (the marshmallow/graham cracker/Hershey bar mess you make around campfires). And you have my word that I will never put bull testicles in your beer, as did the brewers at Wynkoop Brewing Company. They did it as April Fool's novelty, but they got so much attention that it's become a regular part of their product line. Nothing can convince me that the reason Rocky Mountain Oyster Stout sells isn't that guys can dare other guys to try it and get bragging rights if they do. Are these good ideas or marketing hooks? Are they art or the equivalent of a velvet Elvis painting or dogs playing poker?

Aside from bizarre flavors, another gimmick running through the craft brew industry is to raise the alcohol content to ridiculous levels. New Holland's High Gravity Series runs up to as much as eleven percent, more than twice as much as a typical beer. I think that alcohol content beyond that is really undrinkable. Beer flavors are overwhelmed, and the experience of drinking it is more like sipping a liquor. If you want something that powerful, drink a whiskey that controls the flavor profile.

In the end, the consumer will be the judge. If you would rather have pizza beer than pizza with beer, knock yourself out. We won't be brewing it.

Civil Disobedience

Too many of us are out of control.

We are overstimulated by technology. We are surrounded by video screens, and increasingly, video cameras. We carry the Web in our pocket through our smartphones, and are never unplugged from the Matrix that entertains and increasingly controls us. The natural rhythms of our bodies and brains no longer track with the cycles of daylight and dark, nor are they in tune with the seasons. We are drowned in an electronic sea that constantly screams for our attention. On the occasions when we break the surface, we feel naked without the constant bombardment of audio and video messaging. We move too fast, we sleep too little, and our nerves are so frayed by the constant noise and the flood of pixels that we react too quickly, leaving ourselves messes to clean and regrets to bear. Our nervous systems are stressed, and we have forgotten how to give ourselves time to think while breathing slowly and deeply. Our diets are crap: high in calories and low in nutrition, loaded with stimulants and sugars to jack us up and keep us running for a few more hours. Brands have become our new religion with their logos adorning every flat surface around us far more than the religious icons of earlier centuries. It seems that almost every experience or interaction in our lives is branded, trademarked, and tagged for future marketing.

This lifestyle is killing our humanity.

The madness has infected how we eat and drink. Chefs have become like rock stars, another branded experience that keeps us from enjoying the food for its own sake. The craft brewing industry faces the same dilemma: our products are being competitively ranked with brewers boasting about their rankings. It's as if consumers can no longer ask themselves, "Do I like this beer?" Instead, they are obsessed with whether *other* people like it. Social media is supposed to increase our connectedness, but it's making us weirdly unable to form our own opinions and judgments. I watch customers that can't sit and drink a beer without telling everyone on Facebook or Twitter (or whatever the next big thing is) that they're drinking it and posting pictures of the beer that is going flat in front of them while they thumb-type. We've become members of a global Hive Mind, joined by smart phones.

Enough. It's time to stop this madness and taste our effing beer.

A closed bottle of whiskey can be kept for more than 100 years, and it will still be good to drink. After opening, a half-full bottle of whiskey will remain good for five years.

It's time for us to be more deliberate in how we live. As craftsmen and patrons, we should pay more attention to what we're doing and not settle for junk food, junk science, or lives cluttered with junk mail, junk texts, and junk messages on our smart phones, all of them interrupting a quiet beer. We didn't used to be this way. We used to care, to be mindful of what we were doing

STOP
THE
INSANITY,
MAN!!!

because we didn't have all this noise distracting our focus. We didn't need government regulations or clever marketing to remind us to slow down and do it right. We had the time to think and act with intention. The classic science fiction writer and libertarian thinker Robert Heinlein nailed this point when he said, "I believe in the honest craft of workmen. Take a look around you. There never were enough bosses to check up on all that work. From Independence Hall to the Grand Coulee Dam, these things were built level and square by craftsmen who were honest in their bones." How do we recapture those kinds of deliberate standards on ourselves again? Should we not try to brew the best beer our imaginations and abilities allow, even if it isn't going to end up ranked on some website with eighty-three user reviews? Should we not try to appreciate and understand the brewer's art and interpretation without having to Facebook a picture of the glass? When do we all just shut up and drink it?

In fact, Heinlein also pointed the way forward. Forty years ago he was already concerned that our culture was becoming too specialized and shallow. We know how to work our smartphones but not how they work. Too many of us are so enslaved to our technological toys that we have lost the heritage of craft and the capacity to learn multiple skills. Heinlein worried that technology was entertaining us to death and that we weren't as smart and resourceful as we used to be. He worried that we weren't living fully human lives. He said:

> *A human being should be able to change a diaper, plan an invasion, butcher a hog, conn a ship, design a building, write a sonnet, balance accounts, build a wall, set a bone, comfort the dying, take orders, give orders, cooperate, act alone, solve equations, analyze a new problem, pitch manure, program a computer, cook a tasty meal, fight efficiently, die gallantly. Specialization is for insects.*

Most of us can't (or won't) do most of the things Heinlein lists. Technology is our crutch, and over-reliance on it is keeping us from living authentically human lives. Henry David Thoreau, an early nineteenth-century American writer and thinker, argued that there is a fitting life for a human, and if we cannot live it, we will die.

> *I perceive that, when an acorn and a chestnut fall side by side, the one does not remain inert to make way for the other, but both obey their own laws, and spring and grow and flourish as best they can,*

till one, perchance, overshadows and destroys the other. If a plant cannot live according to its nature, it dies; and so a man.

We are not living according to our nature, and Thoreau despaired of what civilization was doing to him. In 1845, a friend referred him to a piece of land owned by their mutual friend, the poet Ralph Waldo Emerson. It was a patch of woods next to Walden Pond outside Concord, Massachusetts. Ellery Channing told Thoreau, "Go out upon that, build yourself a hut, and there begin the grand process of devouring yourself alive. I see no other alternative, no other hope for you." And so he did. He built it with his own hands and lived there for two years, relying on himself and finding what it meant to be fully alive. Afterward, he explained why he did so:

I went to the woods because I wished to live deliberately, to front only the essential facts of life, and see if I could not learn what it had to teach, and not, when I came to die, discover that I had not lived.

I love the way Thoreau strove for an authentically human lifestyle. His writings are so quotable because he talks about the fundamental questions that every man or woman ought to think about, but that we rarely have the peace of mind to consider today. For example, when I think about what all this technology and marketing and media and 24/7 connectedness costs us, I am reminded of Thoreau's point that, "The price of anything is the amount of life you exchange for it."

Stop and taste that quote for a moment. Is Facebook free? Its price tag is the amount of your life you exchange for it. Is all of the marketing and media nonsense that surrounds the craft brewing industry worth it if we cannot just sip our beer in peace?

One of Thoreau's most famous works is *Civil Disobedience,* in which he describes being arrested in 1846 for choosing not to pay his taxes. In it, he reflects Aristotle's notion that, "It is not always the same thing to be a good man and a good citizen." Our country may have gone all in on this overly connected society so that we no longer have private lives outside of the public eye. With law enforcement arming themselves with aerial drones, will we be able to quietly pee while we hike in the woods without Big Brother watching? Sometimes we have to choose to unplug.

Do you want to be bothered and marketed to while you drink your beer? It is an act of civil disobedience to unplug from the Hive Mind. Be deliberate: turn off the phone, or leave it in the car. Drink the beers you like, not what other people tell you you're supposed to like. As Thoreau says in *Civil Disobedience:*

> *I was not born to be forced. I will breathe after my own fashion. Let us see who is the strongest. What force has a multitude? They only can force me who obey a higher law than I. They force me to become like themselves. I do not hear of men being forced to have this way or that by masses of men. What sort of life were that to live?*

Stop the madness, and taste your beer.

The More the Merrier: Celebrate Craft!

We are living through a renaissance of craft brewing and distilling.

Historical forces had already put a huge dent into the craft and artisan heritage of American brewing and distilling when Prohibition came along. The Eighteenth Amendment to the United States Constitution was passed in 1919 and took effect the following year. It prohibited the manufacture, sale, and transportation of intoxicating liquors within (and export from) the United States. Congress then passed the Volstead Act, which limited the alcohol content of any beverage to less than half of one percent. Some breweries made the switch to producing "near beer" that stayed below the legal threshold, but most small operations went bankrupt. Since there is no such thing as "near whiskey," a few distillers started bottling tonics and soft drinks. Most moved operations to Canada or Mexico and focused on serving global markets or the black market in the United States. Prohibition ended in 1933, but World War I, the Depression, and World War II all coincided with innovations in manufacturing, the growth of mass marketing to consumers, and increasing urbanization. The result was a loss of local craft producers of almost everything—small farmers, tailors, and printers were replaced by national producers and chain distribution. We ended up with frozen TV dinners, vacuum-wrapped cupcakes, and canned soda pop.

Beer and spirits were manufactured by a few large corporations, which had consolidated the regional producers. Their advertising efforts didn't *respond* to demand; they *shaped* it. By the 1970s, "American beer" had become a predictable, mild-tasting, watery lager, pasteurized in aluminum cans because that made it cheaper to make, ship on hot trucks, and sit in warehouses or grocery stores for weeks or months. It reduced flavor down to the lowest common denominator in consumer tastes.

At the end of the nineteenth century, beer and spirits reflected regional and local culture and tastes.

My Manifesto

There were hundreds, if not thousands, of variations in small towns and cities. Traditional brewing gave way to six-packs of Bud. Unpasteurized regional beers were considered so unique that in 1977 an entire pop-culture classic movie, *Smokey and the Bandit,* featured Burt Reynolds in a black Trans-Am trying to smuggle a load of Coors from Texas to Georgia within the twenty-eight hour window before it spoiled.

But in the 1990s, the craft revolution was in full swing. There are now over two thousand craft brewers in America, more than there were at the turn of the twentieth century. Is that too many? Can the market sustain this kind of growth?

I say, *Bring it on—the more the merrier!* Let's grow the market, because as big as craft has become, it's still dwarfed by the industrial brewers and distillers. According to industry statistics, in 2011 Americans purchased about two hundred million barrels of beer, of which craft brewers accounted for just under twelve million. There may be a lot of us, but we're still only five or six percent of the market. Our ability to tell the story of craft beer and artisan spirits is dwarfed by the advertising dollars the global industrialists spend.

The craft renaissance is about more than beer and spirits. It includes everything from farmers' markets to mom and pop coffee shops. We're starting to rediscover and care about having a local relationship with what we eat and drink. We are starting to realize that industrialized food and beer is not only cheap, but also cheap-tasting. We want to feel connected to where we live, and we want our restaurants and breweries and stillhouses to connect the farm to the table. We want to be surprised and comforted by local and seasonal flavors. We want chefs, baristas, and brewers to respond to our local culture and concoct things to eat and drink that reflect who we are, not force us to conform to commoditization.

❧ ☙

The Egyptians believed that the god of agriculture, Osiris, taught humans how to make beer.

❧ ☙

At New Holland Brewing, we're working on cultivating a local or regional provenance for our products. We're not far from the day when we will be able to use almost all Great Lakes regional ingredients and achieve more differentiation from national flavor profiles. We want to be distinct and reflect the culture of the Great Lakes region where we brew.

Eventually, I'd like to see brewpubs become like coffee shops, with a distinct community character—one on every busy corner, a place to meet friends and enjoy the neighborhood brew. I'd like to see brewers work with and become like local chefs, cooperating with nearby farmers to integrate beer and food into the seasonal life of the community. Eat and drink what you and your neighbors enjoy. As brewers become more like mom and pop restaurants, it will be interesting to see how many small brewpubs can become viable businesses.

Although many call this a revolution, this movement isn't introducing new ideas. It's a renaissance, a renewed commitment to a more organic culture, and a rediscovery of our cultural roots. I'm thrilled to be a part of it.

What Have You Done with My Beer?!

Imagine you're a parent (some of you don't have to imagine). You have this wonderful child that you've cherished and raised. You've taught him or her to honor your values and carry your family name into the world. You are so proud of your son or daughter. But then the day comes for him or her to leave the nest and move across the country. Your mind fills with what ifs: what if they are mistreated? What if their environment spoils them? What if they try to do the right thing but are misunderstood? It's nerve-wracking because once they walk out the door, you've lost control.

That's the way I sometimes feel about our products. We invest so much of ourselves into creating them. They embody our values and bear our family name. We have such good but specific intentions for how they will be used and what we want people to experience with them. They represent us. And then they leave our loading dock, and we lose all control.

We don't know how our products will be presented on the retailer's shelf. Will it be grouped into the appropriate category so the consumer can find it or understand what it is if they discover it? For example, consider our Belgian *saisson* beer, which most American consumers are not familiar with. If our saisson is stacked next to, say, our competitor's summer wheat beer, it's possible a customer might buy it, expecting a similar product and be disappointed when it turns out not to be what the shelf placement implied.

We don't know what retailers might say about our product if a consumer asks for a recommendation. Has the clerk at the counter ever tasted our product? Under what circumstances? How much do they know about it, and can they answer the customer's questions? We have no idea.

How are our products being served in bars or restaurants? How are servers explaining them? How are they mixing our spirits into drinks or pairing our beers with the food menu? Are they being served at the correct temperature and in the proper glassware which will showcase their features? Again, we have no idea. When they're presented or served in ways we didn't intend, it can reflect badly on us. But we have absolutely no control over the user experience once they leave our dock.

In 1997, Steve Jobs returned to Apple as CEO. One of the first items on his agenda was solving the problem of how Apple products were being sold in the retail space. At the time, Apple was lined up in big box electronics stores next to Microsoft and other competitors with no explanation of how Apple was unique. Store clerks were often poorly trained and couldn't make educated recommendations or answer customer questions. Jobs believed that his products needed their own space that embodied the Apple brand, merchandising that put the products into the right context, and knowledgable staff who could help guide the customer experience.

His solution was to recruit two retail superstars, Millard Drexler, who had been CEO of The Gap, and Ron Johnson, who had been vice president of merchandising for Target stores. With their help, Jobs launched the Apple Store, a chain of retail outlets owned and operated

by the same company that made the products. The result was, in classic business language, a perfect vertical market. Apple would control the product design, the manufacturing, the marketing and distribution, and the retail outlet. Whether you are an Apple fan or not, you have admit that Jobs was able to insure that consumers would get a pure Apple experience. They could control what happened to their babies.

More than 50% of the purchase price of a fifth of whiskey in the U.S. goes to taxes—federal, state and local.

So the obvious question is why we don't do that. Why doesn't New Holland Brewing sell directly to consumers, either with our own stores or chain of restaurants? The simple answer is that we can't because the government won't let us. Welcome to my world.

To explain why, we have to go back to 1919, the year the eighteenth Amendment to the Constitution banned the sale of alcoholic beverages in the United States.

Prohibition lasted fourteen years, until the passage of the twenty-first Amendment repealed the eighteenth (oops, never mind...). The twenty-first Amendment removed federal prohibition but left regulation of the alcohol business up to the individual states. And since it was 1933, the depths of the Great Depression, do you want to guess what most states did? They set up a system that allowed them to not only control alcoholic beverage distribution but to tax every drop of booze at each stage of the supply chain. My state of Michigan, along with most others, created what has become known as the "three-tier system."

The rules are more complicated than you want to know, but the idea is easy to understand. There are three tiers in the supply chain: producers (me), distributors, and retailers (where you buy your Mad Hatter IPA). The state makes sure that the three tiers are completely separate, so a producer cannot sell directly to a retailer. Nor can any tier own another tier. We couldn't, for example, open a chain of New Holland Stores, nor can a chain of restaurants or stores manufacturer their own wine or rum. And, of course, the government has plenty of opportunities to tax transactions at every level. Other than rant and rave, there's nothing that New Holland

Brewing can do about it unless the laws are changed.

Wait, you are saying, *you do have a pub and restaurant where you serve your products?* You may be reading this book inside of it while you drink a Poet Oatmeal Stout. That's because an exception was carved into the three-tier system for breweries and wineries. They can have tasting rooms and sell to consumers on the premises where they produce. Because we have a brew kettle onsite, we are like the tasting rooms at the wineries. We could open another brewpub, but we'd have to produce at least some of our product onsite. But most of our sales are to distributors who in turn sell to retailers who in turn sell to consumers.

The bottom line is that no matter how much imagination and effort we put into crafting a particular beer or spirit, we have very little ability to control the end-user's experience. All we can do is teach about what we do (this book is an example of that), explain ourselves through marketing, and build solid working relationships with our distributors and retailers in which we educate them as best we can about how to present and serve what we produce.

Meeting You Halfway

Can artists put too much distance between their work and their audience? Sure, it happens all the time.

An artist has something to say, but he doesn't want to talk to himself. He wants to be heard, which means that he has to get close to his audience and speak a language that they can understand. It might require effort from the audience to learn a new vocabulary. But a great artist can't be so arrogant that he can't hear what his audience is saying to him. Ultimately, art is a conversation.

For example, the "foodie" revolution has done a great job of starting that conversation. This dialogue has given birth to thousands of amazing local restaurants owned and operated by the chef. They experiment, so sometimes they fail, but the movement has changed the way many Americans think of food. We want creativity, to be surprised by combinations of flavors and textures. More of us are insisting on supporting local economies with local ingredients, and we enjoy our meal more when it is fresh from the farm to the table. We want our food to honor our heritage and reclaim traditional tastes and methods.

Many things have driven the foodie revolution, but it strikes me that a few would be useful for brewers and distillers as well. The first is media like the Food Network channel and shows like *Iron Chef* and *Chopped.* The public has come to think of chefs as creative artists and to expect excellence in innovation. We may not be able to have a game show centered around a timed brewing competition, but to stay sharp, we need to find ways to encourage the public to demand more from us and our products.

The other thing that has helped the foodie revolution make so much progress has been giving consumers the vocabulary to talk about culinary arts. The Food Network and other media have done an amazing job with this. Twenty years ago, very few of us could understand a menu or tell you what went into making our meals. Today, people without any formal training can talk knowledgeably about ingredients and techniques, flavors and traditions. If we could teach our consumers a new vocabulary about beer and spirits, we could communicate more effectively with them about what we are trying to do and what they do (and don't) like. The problem is that while lots of people like to drink our products, they don't have the words to express what they are tasting.

I want people to not only understand and have the vocabulary to be able to discuss what we create, but to actually enjoy it. As much as I've talked about fermenting remarkable art at New Holland, it's important that we create beer and spirits that people can actually drink. It's tempting to take things too far, to think that if a little of something is good—the taste of hops or fruit, for example—then more must be better. Too many craft brewers and distillers are pushing the envelope for no better reason than to get attention. They double (or triple or quadruple) some ingredient as if they were marketing "maximum strength" detergent. Sure, you can make your IPA the most bitter on the market, but why would you? As a marketing gimmick? To get attention, some brewers keep notching up the alcohol content of their beers, so they can claim to be the most potent or adding ridiculous ingredients to produce novelties like cotton-candy flavored vodka. Most of this is unpleasant to drink, except as a goof so you can tell your friends that you tried it.

We have to remember that the point of creating artful beer and spirits is to have a conversation with the consumer; people have to be able to drink it. It should have a signature, make a statement, surprise and educate and teach us something, and do all of that while we drink it. Just as experimental music or fashion can be so innovative that no one can bring themselves to listen to or wear it, beer and spirits that place more value on creativity than drinkability ultimately fail to serve the consumer because they don't have his or her best interests at heart.

The oak barrels give the whiskey its caramel color. By law, no food coloring can be added.

That's why we spend so much time thinking about our beer and spirits. When we brainstorm a new brew,

My Manifesto

we think about its DNA (the tradition that defines it, such as stout, IPA, lager, wheat, etc.), but also about how it might be consumed. We don't just ask how it will taste, but we ask what tastes will go with it. Is it meant to accompany food, or would it ideally be a flavor that stands alone? Would it fit into a meal, or would a meal be built around it? Under what sort of circumstances would we imagine people drinking it? What sort of settings or contexts? For example, Dragon's Milk is not a tailgate-party beer, but a growler of Ichabod is perfect for a football game in the fall.

My point is that we want our beers to take you somewhere, but they should meet you halfway there. We never put novelty above drinkability. Our art will challenge you, but ultimately it is accessible. It might take you out of your comfort zone but only to enlarge that zone. We want to have an enlightened dialogue with you. We want to expand your palate so you can taste more of life, and we want to elevate your *creative palette*, so you can entertain and even educate others to enjoy all that beer and spirits have to offer.

For the Love of the Game

In the early nineties, when I was in college, the craft brewing industry was in its infancy. I remember being impressed and inspired by brands like Sam Adams and Anchor Steam. Maybe it was just because I was so immature and impressionable, but craft brewing felt like a revolutionary act to me, like the release of the first Macintosh computer must have felt ten years earlier. Craft beer has come so far so fast that it might be hard to understand just how different it was from what we expected beer to be. Industrialization and conglomeration had deconstructed the complexity of brewing, reducing its diversity to a boring standard. Beer had become defined in the public's mind as a watery golden lager with a limited flavor profile and low alcohol content. It was the lowest common denominator in consumer expectations that could be made and sold across wide swathes of America.

When I discovered craft beer in college, it opened my eyes to a simple truth: beer could be like food. Just as chefs could infinitely vary the ways they cooked a dish, using their imaginations and responding to local traditions and tastes, beers could be creative and express the brewer's personality. Think about it: how many ways are there to cook an egg? You could visit a hundred restaurants and taste a hundred different interpretations. Beer doesn't have to be like Egg McMuffins: uniform, processed, unsurprising. In the early nineties, a lot of us realized this and seized the opportunity to step up and treat beer as a craft and art. We sold what we had and went deeply into debt to build businesses that let us listen to our muses.

And now, almost twenty years later, we have discovered what success tastes like. There are thousands of craft breweries, tens of thousands of craft beers, and hundreds of thousands of enthusiasts who visit craft beer festivals every year. Millions drink it. And there are millions of dollars to be made. We went from being considered wanna-be-hippies who make our own beer to respected entrepreneurs managing companies with

My Manifesto

hundreds of employees. Back then, we could hardly get an appointment with a banker to ask for a business loan; today, the bankers call us. We get articles written about us, give interviews to the media and are asked to speak to MBA classes. Money, fame, respect—we've arrived.

Now what? We ought to notice the story arc of the Macintosh computer. In less than thirty years, Apple went from an upstart company animated by revolutionary idealism to a corporate behemoth with the power to impose standardization in their industry. I'm an Apple fan, and the company still produces excellent products. But its motivations aren't and can't be the same as when it started. It's not as free to innovate because it has a business to protect. I don't want that to happen to craft brewers. Obviously we no longer have the freedom of the home brewer. But we can't rest on our laurels and be satisfied with how far we've come. We need new blood in the industry, madly idealistic and imaginative revolutionaries who will continue to push the boundaries of the art form. Sometimes there will be misfires and brewers will jump the shark by creating novelty products. But that's the price of innovation.

Our inspiration shouldn't be computers, cell phones, or cars. Those are manufactured products, which are inevitably driven to industrialization in order to achieve quality control and profitability. Instead, we should look to the food industry over the last fifteen years or so. While we were discovering the art of beer and spirits, chefs and restaurateurs were launching a revolution in the culinary arts. They were driven by the same insights: that food had become a boring and unhealthy pattern of chain restaurants and processed foods. They started experimenting with local ingredients, innovating on themes, and rediscovering heritage crafts and traditional methods, all with a commitment to excellence that was wonderfully diverse and experience-driven.

Whiskey gains as much as 60% of its flavor from the type of cask used in the aging.

In the end, we have to ask ourselves why we got into this business in the first place. Of course we wanted to make money—I'm not going to pretend that I was nothing but an idealist, and I certainly don't want to give up my success. But it was more than that. Most of us who started companies like New Holland fifteen or twenty years ago didn't have two nickels to rub together. But if it was *just* a job, there were easier ways to make a living, and none of us really expected this thing to take off the way it did. We loved beer, and we thought we could make better beer than what we could buy in most stores and bars. And as much as we loved drinking it, we loved making it more. We loved the smells, the heat, the physical labor, the science, the planning, the experimentation. We loved coming up with clever names and labels, and we loved tapping a keg and listening to people react when they tasted what we had created.

And now some of us have the opportunity to cash out. The international brewing conglomerates and Big Booze are coming into our industry and offering some of us big checks to sell our brands and walk away. I'm not going to criticize anyone who makes that decision because it's intensely personal. When someone is given an opportunity to give their family some security, maybe for the first time in their lives, we should remember the years of stress they went through covering rent and making payroll. And as idealistic and committed as I am to keeping New Holland as it is, I'm not dumb enough to put into print a pledge that there is not a check big enough to change my mind.

All that being said, we should all be in this to create art in fermented form. Of course we want to be successful, but if we wanted to run *any* kind of business, we could sell our breweries and start carwashes tomorrow. No, we're in it for the love of the game, for the love of the heritage and beauty and possibilities of what we do. I truly believe that we've just begun to discover what beer and spirits can be.

Afterward: What's on Tap?

So, what's next?

I don't exactly know.

However, I do know there's never been a more exciting time to be in this industry. It's an industry that continues to inspire me with people who are equal-parts enthusiastic artist and diligent craft-person. This is a time for innovation, entrepreneurship, and good old-fashioned hard work.

I also know that every day I'm still motivated to contribute to this business and to shift our thinking back to an approach that values passion, connection, and artful purpose. I think we're just beginning to see where this love of art and craft can take us, and I do know that I'm proud to be a part of it.

For my part, I'm going to take my own advice. I'll continue to challenge myself to listen to the thoughtful consumer—the one that cares about what is on their plate and in their glass, the consumer that takes the time to stop and taste. I will push myself to create products that enhance people's lives and that liven conversations. I will hire people who also think that beer is art but who have different ideas about what it takes to create something beautiful.

Sure, when they close the book on me, they might say, "Yeah, he made beer." But just maybe those who share the impassioned journey with me will raise a silent revolutionary fist and say, "No, he didn't make just beer, he made *art.*"

About the Author

Holland, Michigan seemed like an unlikely place to create some of the most innovative beer and spirits in America. But Brett VanderKamp believed that his hometown and the brewing industry were due for a shakeup. He was twenty-four years old when he started the New Holland Brewing Company in 1997 in an abandoned factory with his best friend and $10,000.

In 2012, New Holland was recognized as one of the leading innovators in the craft brew and distilling revolution sweeping the planet. With nearly 150 team members, New Holland's craft beer and spirits are sold in fifteen states, plus Washington, D.C. through a distribution network of nearly fifty wholesalers.

Brett has become a leader not only in his industry but in the community as well, serving on various boards (including the Holland Chamber of Commerce and its Public Policy Committee). He has been the chairman of Jubilee Ministries, a faith-based non-profit working to revitalize Holland's most troubled neighborhoods. He is a founding member, as well as the past president and Government Affairs Committee chairman of the Michigan Brewers Guild, a trade organization for over a 100 small Michigan brewers. In 2011, Brett was honored as one of *Grand Rapids Business Journal's* "40 Under Forty" business leaders.

Made in the USA
Lexington, KY
13 February 2015